Can you play with a ball?

They can play football.

They can play football as well.

They have to get the ball in the net.

He has to hit the ball with a bat.

She has to hit the ball with a bat as well.

She has to get the ball in the net.

He has to get the ball in the net as well.

She has to run with the ball.

She has to hit the ball up over the net.

They have to run and hit the ball.

They have to get the ball in the net.

He has to hit the ball and run.

She has to tap the ball.

Can you play with a ball?

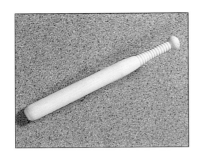

a bat

a ball

a net

a football

run

hit